Born with Pride

Cherishing Family Values

Born with Pride

Cherishing Family Values

Mrs. Martha Ramsey

Mission Possible Press, USA
Extraordinary Living Series

The Mission is Possible.
Sharing love and wisdom for the young and "the young at heart," expanding minds, restoring kindness through good thoughts, feelings, and attitudes is our intent. May you thrive and be good in all you are and all you do...
Be Cause U.R. Absolute Good!

Born with Pride: Cherishing Family Values
by Mrs. Martha Ramsey.

Published by Mission Possible Press
A Division of Absolute Good
P.O. Box 8039, St. Louis, MO 63156
orders@absolutegood.com

Book design by Maureen Cutajar
www.gopublished.com

ISBN 978-0-9852760-3-4

Dedication

This book is dedicated to my children, Regina Ann, Linda Gail, Gregory, Sheila Murelle, Wanda Fay, Paul Cortez, and to my brother Ralph Jones.

I also dedicate this book to the 125 grandchildren, great-grandchildren and great-great-grandchildren that have been born through my children.

Memory Dedication

I thank God for my life, the experiences and the memories. I have seen a lot and would not trade it in for anything. Though at first glance it saddens me to look at this list of those who have gone before me, I am grateful for the love and positivity I continue to have in this lifetime. It is with joy, not sorrow, that I also dedicate this book in loving memory to those who hold a special place in my heart, mind and spirit.

My Children
Wilmer H. Ramsey, Jr., 1950-1958
Mattie Denise Ramsey, 1957-1976
Gregory Ramsey, 1954-2006
Mikel Ray Ramsey, 1956 – 2010

My Grandson Whom We Raised
Terrance LaMonte Ramsey, 1975-1992

My Husband
Wilmer H. Ramsey, 1926-2000

My Mother
K.Z. Smith Jones Nelson, 1907-2003

Contents

Greetings

I started writing this book in 1981. My dear husband never complained about the long hours I put into writing this book. I appreciated his understanding because he knew it was important to me. And as I continued to write throughout the years, my mother continued to encourage me, as she did all my life. I remember when she was living with us at the age of 89 years old, she gave me her love, support and knowledge, as she always did. She said, "Explore your beginning, and share your experiences."

I'm now 82 years old. I didn't begin to finish this book until 2012. It was important to me because this world is too violent, mothers are killing their children, children are acting up and people are forgetting how positive you can be if you have faith, strength and keep moving. Since I've been blessed to live this long, this book could have been well over 300 pages, but I wanted to give you a few things to think about and to use in your life.

If you can learn something from my story that will help you feel better and maybe handle things better in today's society, then this effort has been worth it. You see, with working, being a wife, grandmother, daughter, sister and neighbor, I just didn't have time to finish back then. But I didn't give up.

You've been through some things and will go through more things. Don't give up. I have signs all around my house trying to encourage my grandchildren to live right and make good decisions. Sometimes they listen, and sometimes they don't. I love them anyway. However, there are rules. I know the world is different now, but if they can't follow the rules, they can't stay.

My mother shared things with me that I have been able to pass down to those in my family, and now to you. Be encouraged in your victories and in your tragedies. Have pride and maintain it. When you have pride, you walk tall, you are respectful and you treat others well, with neighborly love. You work hard, you love your family and you live through whatever happens without harming others.

Since it is based on my memory of my past experiences, and many events have been forgotten, perhaps permanently beyond recall, I am usually able to remember the principal experiences of my childhood, youth and adulthood. I hope you enjoy a few of the experiences I have chosen to share. Values and morals are lasting, even when times change.

Cherishing Family Values,
Mrs. Martha Ramsey
St. Louis, Missouri
October 24, 2012

My Mississippi Beginnings

I was born Martha Elouise Jones on April 27, 1930, near a small town called Hazlehurst, Copiah County, Mississippi. I was delivered by a midwife at home, like most of the children that were born in the 1930s. My mother's name was K.Z. My mother says her father gave her that name, but she didn't like it. Can you imagine, a name like that all through life, filled with many years of people asking, “Is that your name?” and, “How do you spell it?” When I was about 15, she decided to change her name to Kay so she could tell people how to spell it.

I never knew my grandmother, Martha Ella Smith, who died before I was born. She had given birth to 16 children during a time when people traveled by horse and buggy. Eleven of her children died from a pneumonia plague, one right after the other. At least three of them died within a week of each other. I think she died of grief.

When I was born, my mother was 23 years old and living at her parents' home, with Grandpa James. The man who raised me, and who I knew to be my father was James Madison Jones, known as "Bunk" to his friends and family. My father loved us all and treated me just like his other children. When I was 15 years old, my mother admitted that she'd had a short affair with my birth father, which had ended before I was born. In fact, I was hurt and angry because I wasn't told about any of it until a woman in the neighborhood said that my birth father was in town and would like to see me.

My father, Mr. Jones, was 40 years older than my mother and had been married before. He had two daughters, and one of them was older than my mother. Together, he and my mother had four boys and three more girls after me.

My father enjoyed fishing, and I loved going out with him and my brothers.
No matter how many people are in the house, cherish your family.

Born Black, With Pride

"Most people that are born black don't want to be black because of the disadvantages against our race, but my mother's father taught her to be proud of being black."
– Mrs. Martha Ramsey

My mother taught us to be proud of being black and a lot of other things. I thought she had all the intelligence. When I needed to know things, I would go to her, and she would tell me how to do it or where to get if from. If she didn't know the information, she knew how to go and get it for me. We had good communication, and I learned from her, trusted her.

My mother taught me hospitality and love at a very young age. When I was growing up we used coal lamps because there was no electricity. In the winter, we had light from the fireplace. I learned that if someone comes to your house, offer them your best and if you're eating, offer them what you have. She said that if there wasn't enough, she would give what was there and eat later. Hospitality is a gift that should be used without grudge.

My grandfather was a preacher, Reverend James Smith, a Holiness Minister from the Church of God and Christ. He was a proud, independent man who owned and ran the family farm near the small town of Hazlehurst, Mississippi. Our family, including extended relatives, lived close by. All of them had some Indian blood, and my mother's mother was a full-blooded Black Creek Indian. They were a proud family.

I'm so glad that my mother listened to her father and passed those beliefs down to me. My grandfather was a very strict man who believed in what he taught and lived everyday by his teaching. I always say that if anyone went to heaven my grandfather was there, too. He loved people, so he was patient and kind. He would go without and put others first to help them; that's what I call longsuffering.

Grandpa James had a motto for living: "Believe in love, have faith, be baptized and you shall be saved." He also said, "Love is being considerate of others." He also said, "Love delights in saying please," and, "Be polite."

"Spot without a wrinkle," is the way he lived his life. In today's language, it would mean, "Do the right thing and practice it." He baptized me when I was about seven years old. I could hear him hum the words, "You better run, run, run and try to make a hundred because ninety nine and a half won't do." That was a song that taught us to do things 100%, spiritually and in life.

Our family did well, loved each other and became skilled in many trades. They were taught to be proud, and they maintained that pride. My aunts and uncles were teachers, preachers, plumbers and seamstresses. Not bad for the Deep South and a time of segregation.

During and After School

Work hard in your profession,
and color or race won't make a difference.
Pride is the key to success in life.

As my mother was growing up in the Deep South, the slavery mentality was very evident, especially in those days. Yet, my grandpa was recognized in his community as a proud man who stood up for his family. He had his own farm and took care of it himself--stock and all. The children helped him farm the land, and he took care of them, himself and the livestock. He would not hire his kids out to white farmers for money. Nor would he allow his wife to clean and cook meals for "white folks," although they would ride by on big horses and ask him many, many times. He told them his wife and girls had all they could do at home. So they respected his statement and went on their way saying, "Okay, Uncle Jimmy."

When I was growing up, a child could register for school at five years of age. My mother was anxious to get me in school, and I was happy about starting school. Our farm was about nine miles east of Hazlehurst, and we lived three miles from Sardis Grade School. So my mother arranged for me to stay during the week with the teacher, Miss Clara Green, who had also been my mother's teacher when she was young. Miss Clara, along with her nieces and nephews, lived in a very big old house that her relatives left her located near the school.

What a bad experience, living at Miss Clara's house. Her nieces and nephews would take me to the house and beat me. They dared me to tell any of the grown-ups what they were doing to me. Oh, was I glad when the weekends came. My mother would walk and get me on Friday afternoon and bring me back on Monday morning. This happened until my brother, Rufus, was old enough to go to school, and then we walked the three miles to school together each day. Although I loved school, the kids would get into fights along the way. I promised myself that when I grew up, I would even the score with those kids as soon as I was big enough. Tears came from my eyes because I didn't like to see anyone hurt.

Speaking of being hurt, my brother, Rufus, and I were responsible for getting the water that our family used in the house. I remember one day my mother sent us to get water, and Rufus fell into the spring. That frightened me so much, I haven't forgotten it. My brother crawled out of the spring, and we ran home. That day, we did not get the water until my father came home from work.

Many times, to make it through, I said, "Father, give me courage to make it through this day. I stretch my hands to Thee, no other help I know."

With faith in God, education and an occupation,
believe in yourself.
Be confident in your ability, and hold your
head high.

Wonders of Nature

When I was growing up, many things took place. It was during the Depression years that my mother worked for the Works Progress Administration (WPA). The WPA was created by President Franklin D. Roosevelt to employ unskilled workers to provide food and basic essentials as part of the New Deal. My father worked on the farm.

I remember the dogwood trees that blossomed in the spring were so beautiful. We got our water from the well, which was connected to our house. There was a creek about a mile down the pasture, and close to it was a water spring. I can remember the white sand at the bottom of the spring, the water tasted so good and I enjoyed it so much more than the well water that was closer to our house.

One fall day our house caught on fire. It burned down, and we lost everything. We had no insurance on our home or its contents. We went to live at the Lewis family home, who were friends of my mother. We lived there until my dad found us another home. They were so nice to us, yet their children were a bit mean to us. I'm not sure if they felt their parents were favoring us, or they felt that we were in their "territory," and that's the reason they acted that way. I could not be happy in someone else's home, so that was an unhappy stay.

Dad and Mom bought her eldest sister's farm from her husband because she had died while delivering her seventh child. That farm adjoined my grandfather's farm. When I was 11, he died and mom got his farm, too. Comprised of two inherited farmhouses, our house was big with big oak trees in the back yard for shade. I love flowers, and we had plenty of those, too. On hot summer days, my parents and we children would sit on our back porch. On warm nights, we watched the stars and the moon from the porch, which extended from one end of the house to the other. I always enjoyed sitting, talking and playing there.

Being the eldest of eight children, I loved living on the farm but was no good at doing farm work. So my mother would have me to do mostly housework, and she would work out in the field. With my three sisters and four brothers, we helped our parents take care of our home and farm. I enjoyed milking the cows and gathering eggs. Looking for ginney nests was a real trip. The ginney, similar to chickens, were speckled and looked like they were wearing polka dot dresses. They could not be tamed, so they hid their nests. Trying to find these secret hiding places was an adventure for me. From our house, I went out into the pasture. I had to go and look in the high grass because that's where they hid their nests. I also had to wait and watch them until they left the nests because they would peck if you tried to take their eggs. I was hunting those eggs because I thought they would have speckled eggs that looked like them! I kept searching, but all the eggs I found looked just like regular hen eggs, white with no speckles.

My father was a very industrious man. He had a lot of pride, too. He grew a little cotton that he would take to the mill and then sell at the market. His biggest crops were the vegetables for the market and home. We grew tomatoes, corn, potatoes, sweet potatoes, squash, okra, cabbage, onions, turnips, sweet peas, string beans, mustard greens, collard greens, butter bean, pole bean, peanuts, watermelon, cantaloupe, even sugar cane and sorghum for syrup used for popcorn.

He would grow and sell cabbage by the ton at the market, about 15 miles away. It was on big trucks. We didn't have phones then, so there were times when the market didn't need more cabbage, and he would have to take it back because he couldn't sell it. During those times, they would unload the whole truck on the side of the road, and the people who needed it would just get it for free.

I liked to tag along with my brothers and father when they went fishing. I just enjoyed seeing him catch fish. He was a good fisherman. I would pick the ripe berries and wild flowers along the way. Sometimes while we were out fishing and walking, we would get caught in big storms with lightning and thunder. The lightning and thunder frightened me. My father would get us all under some sort of shelter. We could usually tell when it was going to start raining because it seemed like the fish would start biting real good just before the rain started. It was fun and exciting, and we would be all wet when we arrived home.

I never will forget the time I tried to catch a humming bird that kept flying around the flowers. I closed the flower up, with the humming bird inside it, and it stung me with his long bill. It hurt so badly.

There were so many things to do around our home and in our community that kept us happy and occupied. We had horses, pigs and hunting dogs, in addition to the chickens and cows. I also looked forward to going on trips during summers with my mother, brothers and sisters. We would ride the bus and sometimes the train to visit my father's relatives and mother's cousins in Bogalusa, Louisiana.

We lived in hilly country where there was red clay, dirt rocks and sand. There were many different trees like oak, pine, hickory and sweet gum. We had a peach orchard, fig trees, and red and yellow plum trees. There were nut trees, mulberry trees, blackberry vines, little huckleberry trees (which look like today's blueberries), dewberry bushes that grew close to the ground and gooseberries too. All of these grew wild in those woods. It was fun to go pick nuts and berries when they were ready. The food was nutritious and didn't cost anything. Oh, the wonders of nature.

As a small girl, I can remember being very happy with loving parents and a good home. Our parents were proud, and they never mentioned being poor to us children. When we grew up, we didn't know anything about poor; we just didn't have any money.

Preserving the Family and Our Food

I enjoyed my parents' cookouts in the backyard. They included roasted corn in shucks and boiled green peanuts from the fields. They would wash the dirt off the peanuts, put on an iron pot filled with water and add a little salt. The peanuts were not shelled, and they would boil until done. I loved those peanuts.

In those days, we didn't throw away anything. Mother cooked chicken feet and dumplings, and father loved that dish. Mother took pride in a good peach cobbler, a perfect bed of zinnia flowers or a neatly pieced quilt block. The total of many little things made her happy. I remember the happiness I felt one morning when the fruit orchard had burst overnight into bloom and the day when the creek through my parents pasture swept banks full of water after an April downpour.

I remember crepe myrtle bushes in full bloom and when autumn's glorious colors crept across the hillside. Sweet potatoes roasted in the hot ashes of the hearth were fit for a king, as was corn on the cob. "You don't need money to be rich," mother would tell me. "God made heaven and earth, and all things are His. The flowers, the birds, the animals, the trees and the fruits of the earth are all yours free to feast your eyes on whenever you like, and no one can take them from you."

My mother and father would take us for walks on full moon nights. We kids would catch lightening bugs in jars along the way as we listened to the frogs croak. The roosters would crow and wake us up every morning. On Saturdays, Mom and Dad would take the wagon into town for supplies while we kids stayed at home and did our chores. My brother cleaned the yard, and I did the ironing.

My mother used to make homemade bars of soap. I didn't get that recipe, so I'm not sure what she used to make it. I do know that she boiled the clothes in a large black pot outside in the yard. And when she put the clothes on the line to dry, the white clothes were really white, and the colored clothes were bright. She also made our clothes. I always preferred that she sew my clothes rather than buy them from a store. My mother could make everything to fit me so well.

I liked harvesting time. After school we had to pick the peanuts off the vines and take the corn to the mill to grind up for cornmeal. We cut the sugar cane and took it to the mill to make syrup. We also grew sorghum that we took to the mill to make sorghum molasses. We had a smokehouse where my father would cure the meat. When he killed the hogs, I ran away because I hated to hear the sound of them squealing when they hit them on the head. That was life on the farm, and I enjoyed the bacon, sausage and ham, all of which would hang along the walls. My father cooked the lard in a big black pot and made crackling. I liked to eat them and crackling bread, which is crispy pork rinds baked inside of cornbread.

Mother canned, or preserved, fruit and vegetables a lot for our family. From peaches, pears, huckleberries, blackberries, plum jelly, beans, corn, tomatoes, apples, cucumbers and beets, the food was plentiful. And we did this to preserve it for the winter. They even dug a hole in the ground big enough to have a door to go down and lined it with straw where we banked potatoes to keep during the cold season.

Christmas time was a real joy. A boy named Junior Patterson gave my first manicure set to me at a Christmas party at school. I always disliked him because he called me "Halloween" since my middle name is Elouise, and he could not pronounce it right. On the day before

Christmas, every year my family and I went out and cut down a holly tree to decorate. Oh, what fun. We made all of our decorations. We saved the silver off of gum wrappers throughout the year for icicles. We made different color chains of string from construction paper. We always had plenty to eat and a few toys on Christmas. When I was small, I really thought Santa came down the chimney with his sack of toys.

Changing Seasons

My parents had certain rules around the house. Like, whenever it was thundering or lightening, we did nothing but sit in a corner until it was over. My mother would say a little prayer. Another rule in our home was that six days we labor, the seventh day we were to rest. No washing, no mending, no ironing, no cleaning and no fieldwork, only cooking the family meal on Sundays. We went to church every Sunday. After church, Mother read a lot, and we all relaxed. During the winter months, we would enjoy sitting around the fireplace, listening to nighttime ghost stories, anecdotes about Negro slaves, Indian folktales and all types of folklore Mother would tell us. We listened to experiences about our fore fathers, some of whom were slaves.

My father seemed very happy with plowing his fields, caring for his animals and taking care of the crops. He wasn't a very talkative man but loved his family and provided for us. Independent and proud, he was; he liked horseback riding, hunting and fishing. My father never ate catfish. He would throw them back in the water if he caught one. He just didn't like the idea that the catfish were scavengers. I often think about the things he would bring back from hunting trips--possums, coons, rabbits and squirrels. I did not like to eat coons; they looked like dogs to me.

My mother made many sacrifices for us kids. She was not what you would call a sentimentalist and never did a lot of kissing the family. She was, in appearance, unemotional and silent, yet she gave us much love and attention. I never heard her say, "You kids get on my nerves," "I am tired of you all," or "I need to go away for awhile." Never did I hear those statements from either of our parents. My mother would teach us to talk with good English, have good manners, respect other people and their property, act and walk with pride and be obedient. Her gentle philosophy and her unwavering faith have kept me going through the years from day to day.

I come from a proud family, and my parents wanted things right. As the oldest girl, my mother wanted me to learn how to play the piano. She wanted me to have those types of skills, so she sent me to a music teacher for lessons. My parents bought me an organ, but it got harder and harder every week. My interest in music faded, and I finally gave up and stopped taking lessons. Everything has a season.

Living in the country as a child, life was more carefree and peace-filled, so I never knew about violence. It wasn't necessary to lock our home if we forgot to latch the screen door. No one would bother us through the night. There just wasn't much of a need for locks on houses, cars or bicycles. If anyone killed each other, I never heard my parents speak of it. Even the many books Mother bought for us had good things to read about. They were about loving, caring, being honest, being obedient and being happy. I don't even remember hearing my parents gossip or say bad things about anyone.

When we had a bad year with the crops, they always look worried but never discussed those things around us kids. When I was 15 years old, my mother and father sold their farm and moved to the edge of the town. My father was getting old and sick, and they had not done so well on the farm for a few years. They bought two acres of land and built a house.

As I grew older, I realized what advantages I had as a child. Parents and children should not suffer for food, shelter and clothing. They should be able to participate in different activities at church, school or elsewhere.

Learning skills helps to shape the lives of children and prepares them for adulthood.

City Living

Once we moved off the farm, things were a lot different. We didn't even have a garden. My mother started working at the box factory in town. She got me a job with her, so in the evening after I finished school we went to work together from 3pm to 11pm. That was hard on me trying to stay awake in school after working at night. But still, my mother encouraged me to stay in school and get an education. "Be proud, hold your head up high and have good morals in life," I can

Wilmer H. Ramsey, Young Soldier, United States Army

still hear her say. I always tried to do as my parents taught me because I thought they knew best for me. They were adults, so they had already experienced life and its trials and tribulations. Also, they lived for us children and wanted the best for us.

In those days, most young ladies were taught to get married and have a family, not about going to college and having a career. At an early age my mother taught me to do things that would help when I became a woman. Besides the basics like ironing, cooking, cleaning and sewing, I also learned to do needle work like embroidery and crochet. Knowing how to can fruit and vegetables, how to preserve jellies, and how to milk the cow then churn the cream for the butter were all important in order to survive and continue to exist.

When I was 17, I was in my last year of high school and I got married with the consent of my parents. My husband, Wilmer Ramsey, was 21 years old when we got married. I had only known him for one month, and I had never gone steady with any boys. I wasn't pregnant or anything. We were just ready to be married, and everyone was happy for me.

It all started one day when my mother sent my brothers, Rufus and Roosevelt, and me to the store. There was a tall young man at the meat counter. He caught my eye, but I didn't want him to see me looking at him so I pretended not to notice him. My mother taught me that it was impolite to talk to a boy first. He came up to me smiling and winking his eye. I blushed and looked down. He asked me my name and if he could walk home with me and take my groceries home. I said yes, with my two brothers tagging along.

I liked Wilmer a lot at first sight, and he was very nice and polite. We went to the movie theater together the next week. Right after that, I took my younger brothers to their elementary school for a play, and he also took his sisters. He had just been released from the Army, and though I had never met him, all of the teachers and parents there remembered him and begged him to play the piano. He played that piano. That boy could play it so well, and it really touched my heart, although I pretended it was nothing. It was raining outside so when everyone was ready to leave, he offered me his

Mr. and Mrs. Wilmer H. Ramsey, Restored Wedding Photo

umbrella since he couldn't escort me because he had to take his sisters home. I went along with the other kids and my cousins that I came with.

My husband had gotten a job at the Hazlehurst Box Factory. For the first six months of our marriage we lived with my parents, and then they moved back to Louisiana. A year later we had our first baby girl, Regina, and then he and I moved into this little two-room house, and we were so happy because he had gotten us a place of our own. I would take care of the baby and cook our meals. It was heavenly. My husband's parents didn't live far from us. We always enjoyed our visits with them because they were so nice and proud. His mother loved playing her big piano. Wilmer also had seven brothers and sisters, so we were surrounded by family, his and mine.

Moving Beyond Tragedy

While we were still living in Hazlehurst, my first son, Wilmer Jr., was born. The next year we moved to Baton Rouge, Louisiana. My husband found a job working for a grocery store. We were very happy, and we liked Baton Rouge very much. We would go fishing on the bayou and lakes every other weekend. My husband's brother, Robert, lived there too. He sang with a quintet, a group of five. He would take my husband with him when they went to practice. This was around 1953, and they would sing at churches in small towns

Martha Ramsey, Young Wife and Mother

like New Roads, Platinum, Scotland and also Zachary, all in Louisiana. Robert really wanted Wilmer to join in their group; however, he wasn't really into singing.

Soon my husband started working at the Ideal Cement Plant in Baton Rouge. We had five more kids there, Linda, Gregory, Michael, Denise and Sheila. As a family we enjoyed the parks and the carnival with the children, as well as the theater. On Sundays we always went to church. I liked going to events at Southern University. We moved from the city of Baton Rouge to the suburbs. Every year the cement plant had a big picnic in the park for employees and their families with ice cream, hotdogs, barbecue and horse back rides, and we really enjoyed those times.

The children took the bus to school. On March 10, 1958, when Wilmer Jr. was seven years old, a car hit him when he was crossing the street to get on the bus. I just wanted to die when the nurse said he was dead. I was 27 years old. I blame myself because that fatal morning he did not want to go to school. I told him he had to go. It was horrifying, and I could not eat or sleep for a week.

Through prayer, faith and trust in God, my husband and I were given relief. One day I thought to myself, "What about my other children?" They had to be taken care of. I prayed for God to help me overcome my grief. As I read the daily paper, I saw that lots of people were losing their loved ones every day. Sons, daughters, mothers, fathers, sisters and brothers were each passing. Life still had to go on. I can never forget him because he was my child and a part of me. It depressed me very much and though I kept going, the pain in my heart would not go away. It got better when I found out I was pregnant with my daughter, Sheila, who was born July 20, 1959. I had heard that if you are feeling down or depressed it would have a bearing and effect unborn children, so I had to make some choices, and I did.

You must think outside yourself and consider others whom you love, especially during times of grief. Tragedy happens, and we must learn to keep going, cherishing, too, those who are still living.

Our Missouri Migration

In 1960, the Ideal Cement Plant laid off many of the workers, including my husband. When that happened, we moved to St. Louis, Missouri, where my uncle, Gayley Smith, my mother's brother, was living and managing an apartment building at the time. My father had passed in 1954, leaving my mother a widow with three of my younger sisters still in school. Since mother had decided to make the move to Missouri, we thought moving there would be good for us all. We were able to move our family into the building that my uncle managed. They had an Ideal Cement Plant in St. Louis, too, and we were hoping Wilmer would get a job there. But it didn't happen. My husband was looking for employment for a while, and we were having a very hard time, although we were blessed with a place to live.

So many people were unemployed, and times were rough. My husband drew unemployment until it ran out. It got harder, and my husband had to sell our car

Mother and Martha at Goodfellow Blvd. in St. Louis

for food for the kids. Now we had no transportation. Jobs were very hard to find. We kind of lived from day to day, hoping for a break. Finally, my husband got a job at Jack Evans doing industrial work. The job was temporary and soon ended. We didn't know how we were going to pay the rent. When we left Baton Rouge, the company had told my husband they would send for him when they started rehiring at the cement plant. We were hoping they would call any day.

On March 2, 1961, my daughter, Wanda, was born while we were living on Olive Street. I did not like living there because it was an apartment, it was small and the environment did not feel like home. In Baton Rouge we lived in a house. In 1962, we moved out in the West End on Cabanne Street, and though it was also an apartment, it was much better. My husband was doing odd jobs to feed us and keep a roof over our heads. On June 6, 1963, we had my son, Paul. I was very upset because my husband had not found full-time employment, and we needed food and shelter. I had to send my baby home while I was still hospitalized. I was very sick, as he was my ninth and final child. My mother was living across the street when Paul was born. She and my husband had a hard time with that little boy while I was in the hospital for a month. Once I got out of the hospital, the landlord wanted us out since we were unable to keep up with our rent. We moved to a less expensive apartment a couple of blocks over.

In 1965, my husband got into a retraining program started by President John F. Kennedy. About a year later, I started work at St. Luke's Hospital. We were able to start building after that. Participating in that program, along with my husband's full-time job at Mirax Chemical Company, allowed us to start saving.

In February 1968, we bought our first home. It was a 5-bedroom, 2-story brick home. Our address was 5972 De Giverville. Many of our children were big, and some had finished high school. I was so glad we had enough room for our children because we had a big family. In the summer we had parties out on the back patio, lots of food, dances and games.

That same year, my daughter, Linda, graduated from modeling school. When she was offered a job in New York, we were afraid to let her go. We were kind of old-fashioned, and she was still in high school. We just felt that she was too young to venture out on her own into a big city like that. Going out there was green to me, too, and since I had other children, I couldn't leave. So she let that go. My son, Gregory, went into the Army, and Michael went into the Air Force.

Everything seemed to be going so well for us all, and our children were doing fine.

The 1970s

My father, Mr. Jones, died in 1954. Remember, he was 40 years older than my mother. She had always said that by the time all of her children had gotten grown, she would remarry. In 1972, she married Hester Nelson, who was a widower living in Memphis, Tennessee. He had started visiting St. Louis regularly because he had a grown daughter and grandchildren that he was getting to know. Yes, if you haven't guessed it, we had a special relationship... My mother married my birth father when I was 42 years old. After he had visited

Mr. and Mrs. Hester Nelson, My Parents

my hometown when I was 15, I didn't have much contact with him. He had a wife and a few children. They didn't live in the same rural area where we were living. After I got married and moved to St. Louis and his wife died, I started to build a relationship with him. He was a very, very nice gentleman. My birth father took my mother, now his new wife, to his home where they shared a home together for few good years before he passed.

My mother and father opened Nelson's Care Home for the elderly in Memphis. Their motto was "Behold I have set before you an open door which no man can shut" (Rev. 3:8). She and my father operated their business by themselves. My mother always wanted to help others. When her oldest brother took sick, she came to St. Louis and took him home to Memphis with her. She and my father cared for him until he died. Every summer we took the children to Memphis to visit my parents. We enjoyed summer evenings down on Beale Street, watching people sing and dance on the outside. Bands playing all over the place, and it was great fun.

On February 29, 1976, in St. Louis, tragedy struck once again. A man murdered my 18-year-old daughter, Mattie Denise Ramsey. My brother had dropped her off at our house. Evidently, the boy she had been seeing at the time was upset with her and was hiding in the shrubs, waiting on her to come home. He stabbed her and severed the main artery in her groin. My husband was home but was asleep. My little ones heard noise but didn't know what was happening, and they were afraid when they heard the commotion. It was horrifying because she tried to go up the stairs to her room to make it to her babies, Pamela and Nicole, who were ages two and one. Blood was all over the floor and in the foyer on the walls leading upstairs. She bled out in a matter of minutes.

I was at work on the midnight shift at St. Luke's Hospital. I had to go down to the emergency room for some supplies. And as I entered, there were police and detectives all over the place. I heard one of the officers say they had a homicide. I turned and saw my daughter on the stretcher with an airwave in her mouth, lying very still with her hair roller still in her hair. I just asked God to have mercy on me, to help me through the pain and suffering and to give me endurance.

Everyone at work was so wonderful. They gave me much support, as did my neighbors who were so nice, but it hurt so much.

My husband and I had to go on with our lives; we still had children to raise. Two years after our daughter's murder we sold our house because we had bad memories. We bought a three-bedroom ranch style house in the suburbs of St. Louis. I traveled back to the city to work at St. Luke's for one year. Then I started working at Christian Hospital Northeast because it was closer to where I was living. When we bought the house my brother, Roosevelt, was sick with lung cancer. He got sicker that April, and he died, so that left my mother with seven children, four girls and three boys.

We raised our granddaughters, Mattie's children, as our own for about 10 years. When I was set to have surgery, my mother took them and had them with her in Memphis for about three years. I was glad they were able to get to know her and be influenced by her. My mother was pretty old and eventually, they moved back to St. Louis with my daughter, Wanda. That was good because she was younger and had the energy to deal with raising teenagers and all that came with that.

During those hard times, I continued to look to my mother for moral support. She would always come with her love, advice and confidence in me, her daughter. She would say, *"Girl you can't give up! Oh, no. No matter how hard life may seem, take pride and hold your head high. Ask God for endurance because you can weather the storm. Have faith and trust in yourself. Keep your mental attitude at all times. Have courage, confidence, enthusiasm, because this journey in the world is not easy."*

I think back to that night we lost Mattie. We had gone to the store, and she had planned to cook dinner that next night. She had washed her hair and put rollers in it, and it was happy that night.

Spring 1983

I continue to enjoy eating fresh food and the bounty of nature. I am old-fashioned, drink plenty of water, and I wash my hair and let it dry naturally overnight. I remember April 12, 1983. It had been raining everyday that month. I had gotten the flu and was improving slowly, looking forward to my doctor's appointment so she could tell me when I could return to work. As I was healing, concentrating on my garden helped me. My flower bushes, lilac trees, jonquil (yellow flowers), turnips and peach trees had been blooming for two weeks. My lettuce, collards and mustards were all up and growing well. The children didn't follow me out to the garden; it was quiet and I could think. They stay away because they didn't like the worms and the bugs. Yes, I still have a garden, and I get relief from walking around in it.

While resting quietly, I thought of my little son that was run over by a car when he was seven, my daughter that was murdered at 18, and my dear brother who died of lung cancer at the age of 43. He broke our chain of eight children born to my mom and dad. I was weeping silently May 10th. I had been back to work for two weeks, getting stronger everyday, thanking God for my job. My husband started working 10 hours a day, and my son, Gregory, had returned from the Army and joined his dad, also working at Mirax Chemical. I received a lovely letter from my mother that day also.

That spring brings other fond memories. I'll never forget that day in the hospital lobby where I was working, I saw a 97-year-old man clad in high boots with a cowboy hat walking straight upright. I was 53 years old at the time. He bore no wrinkles in his face, which was amazing, and he was very alert. He was driving, too. He didn't look like anything was wrong with him, no arthritis or any of those things that tend to happen as we age. It just struck me how amazing life can be.

Nature for me has often filled in certain spaces in my life. I never was a person who had a close girlfriend, I think because I had my husband and so many children. Whereas a lot of people could sit down over coffee and talk about things with someone they trust, I just never took on that one. I tried to get along with everyone, and I never was into gossiping and such, just kept it at a distance. There were always so many things going on with us, I wasn't interested in that and didn't have time for it.

It's important that we know that we are connected. We cannot go beyond God's reach or beyond His love and care. For we are all a part of God, God is everywhere and through His love we communicate and we live. I could do my work all day without complaints, being thankful for having a job, healthy children and my loving husband.

Women's Rights in the 1980s

I joined ROWEL, which stood for Reform Organization of Welfare. Members of the St. Louis religious community wanting to advocate for the poor and to change the welfare system established ROWEL in 1972. My first trip to Jefferson City was on Tuesday, May 24th 1983, and it cost me $15.00. The North County legislators sponsored the bus trip to the Capitol building, where The House of Representatives and the Senate meet. Each bus had 46 passengers, and there were five buses. They passed out a breakfast pack on the bus and served us a hot lunch overlooking the Missouri River at Ellis Porter Park. Our bus left North County at 7:15 am, and we returned around 6:00 pm. That was the first of many trips.

We would go to Jefferson City to lobby for rights, especially for women's and mothers' rights. Those trips were interesting. I learned about Congress and how bills are passed. I also got a chance to meet a lot of the senators, representatives, and even the Governor, and I got to see the Governor's Mansion.

The Governor's Mansion has color all around the ceiling with gold leaves, Victorian-style furniture, and very old chandeliers that were gas before they were converted to electric. The shutters on the windows are ivory. Posts are marble and gold. Large mirrors with gold trim hang above the mantel. A piano by Steinway, a sunroom and a dining room that has an old large table and chairs are stunning. Embroidered dogwood flowers on red velvet wallpaper with gold leaves and edging, along with wooden dividing doors also fill the home.

Most people on the legislative trip were talking about the high cost of taxes, food inflation, excessive government spending and wasteful government programs. Some people think our government is treating its citizens about the same way the King of England treated our people before the Revolutionary War. They think our public officials should take the time to read the Declaration of Independence frequently. I share this thinking because we should know what it says, as United States citizens.

Our Declaration of Independence states: We hold these truths to be self-evident, that all men are created equal, that they are endowed by their Creator with certain unalienable Rights, that among these are Life, Liberty and the pursuit of Happiness, --That to secure these rights, Governments are instituted among Men, deriving their just powers from the consent of the governed, --That whenever any Form of Government becomes destructive of these ends, it is the Right of the People to alter or to abolish it, and to institute new Government, laying its foundation on such principles and organizing its powers in such form, as to them shall seem most likely to effect their Safety and Happiness. (US 1776) I agree.

Meeting Walter Mondale in Jefferson City, who was a presidential candidate in 1984, was okay. However, I had already chosen my candidate. I was for his opponent, Reverend Jesse Jackson for the Democratic nomination. These trips and activities were important to me because the bills that are passed or not passed affect families. If we don't know the process, or don't even know that they exist or the impact the legislation has, we are powerless to affect change and to have more rights for our society and families. I think everyone should learn these things, participate in the process and vote.

Today, there are so many women who are raising their children, and they have no idea that the bills for which we were lobbying were for their protection, rights and resources. We helped pass laws that help not only support stronger foundations, but also encourage getting financially stable through working.

Homeless Women

I have read many stories of people's pain, hunger and suffering as a result of homelessness. The *St. Louis Post-Dispatch* newspaper ran an article in 1983 on a nurse who befriended "bag ladies" to study the lives of homeless women in Philadelphia. The study found that some of the women liked being independent and felt free of structure and of the social system that they found overwhelming. They didn't like to be called bag ladies, as they were resilient survivors and smart women, as described by the writer.

Adept at negotiating, the writer called them "Box Ladies" because they sleep on cardboard boxes over heated grids or in big boxes. They don't like to be put in categories or labeled. They like to be called ladies. They feel that gives them protection, that people will treat them nicer. If that does not work, they employ other strategies; for example, they will deliberately wear urine soaked clothing or other very soiled clothes. They feel those bad odors would keep anyone away that is thinking of harming them. They also fear men.

According to the writer's research, the ladies are vying for the same food and shelter as the homeless men. The only homeless women she saw with men were the alcoholic women among the bag ladies. The average age of these transient Philadelphians was between 45 and 55. Most had more than one shopping bag, and they kept them in lockers in train stations and department stores. The lockers belong to their friends who were cleaning women in the train and bus stations and clerks in the department stores. In these bags they carry many useful and unusual items; for example, they usually have clean underwear an extra dress, stockings or an extra jacket because there are many pockets to put things in.

They usually carry many paper towels, too, and milk, bread and fruit to snack on during the day. Most eat only twice a day. Breakfast about 5 am and dinner about five pm. These women know what it is like to be cold and have aching feet, says Ms. Strasser. She noted bad teeth and swollen legs that become ulcerated as the two worst health problems facing these women. The leg swelling and ulcers come from never having a chance to put their feet up. They are not permitted to do this in trains and bus stations where they seek shelter. These women suffer from sleep deprivation. For many, sleep comes in snatches and snoozes in the department store lounge, in the library, in the churches that open for all day masses and in the train station. For a few hours at night before they are chased out by cleaning crews or in bus stations were they also can stay for just a few hours.

One woman slept in a telephone booth. The ladies have a very low opinion of social workers and those in the health care field, she says. They said that they hated social workers, doctors were no good and nurses probed and pried and asked too many questions. But they accepted this instructor at the Maryland School of Nursing, who became one of them, to write a Master's Thesis on shopping bag ladies. She told them she was a nurse and was writing down their story so that others would know about their life. And when they gathered for their goodbyes, they gave her gifts, including a new blue blouse from the trash, an old newspaper and a pen that would not write.

Homeless men have been researched to death, but no one had studied homeless women. She contends her mission now is the heightened the awareness of others to the simple needs of these women: food and shelter. She gave an intimate view of this special population to graduate nursing students who may have to help these women some day. She also hopes to interest others in plans to seek funding from the state legislature to expand the services offered to the increasing numbers of homeless women.

When reading the article, I was surprised to learn how they survived on the streets, and I was surprised at how they lived, what they did to make it and how they protected themselves. A lot of these women were family women who had lost jobs, had gotten divorced, suffered mental illnesses or fell on hard times of some kind. What happens in our society affects us all. The plight of any person without a home is a problem. I thank God that these women and others who have hard times have learned to be reliant on their skills and themselves to make it. Don't give up hope.

Finances

When people believe they are poor or that they don't have enough, it effects everything. The way people think, behave and their attitudes. During my lifetime I have seen crime on the rise, folks losing homes, schools getting worse and people losing their minds. This is not what our society is supposed to be like. We are to have pride and care about ourselves and others. I know it's tough, but it's up to us to take a stand and make it. Having good jobs and financial stability are so important.

Financial stability and security is one of my goals. It has been important to me since I started to learn about it at 55 years old. As a young girl my parents were trying to care for eight kids with their low income. They taught us to be honest, obedient, finish school, get a job and have a family after marriage. They never said anything about saving for retirement or making financial goals. They were farmers, so buying their farm, caring for the stock and hoping for a good crop every year was their basic plan.

The first 20 years of my marriage, we had low paying jobs and a very big family. My husband and I, with five girls and four boys, were most concerned with food, clothing, shelter and transportation. Buying a home for our children and living one day at a time was our life. I had not really thought of our retirement while we were trying to meet car payments and mortgage payments. We worked hard to pay the gas, lights, telephone and water bill each month.

I had been working at Christian Hospital Northeast for six years when my schedule was cut down to two days a week. We had to make ends meet so I started to work for Kelly Health Care Services, part-time in private duty, as a Nurse Aid. On August 27, 1985, I received my commission for a notary. I was sworn in a few months later and took my oath as a Notary Public. For 15 years, I had wanted to become a Notary Public so that I could provide a service to my community, and now it had been fulfilled. I also set that year as a goal to finish my book, this book that you are reading, but with working and grand children I just did not have time.

On November 25, 1985, I received a call from Memphis from my sister, Mildred, who told me that her six-year-old granddaughter had just died of a highly infectious childhood disease. At the time, I was on my way back to Jefferson City with two other ladies to the state capitol for ROWEL. We were lobbying to pass a bill on the Medicaid allowance, which is critical to meet basic needs of people who are uninsured. I had to encourage my sister to be strong and give support to her daughter. I could not go to the funeral but after getting my adult children together, we decided who could get off work and go. My mother was living in Memphis and as always, she gave her love and encouragement with prayers to the family.

If you don't save for retirement, you won't have anything for emergencies. You can't even borrow money these days like we used to be able to do. You have to depend on yourself. Emergencies happen, and hopefully you will be blessed with a long life. We say we don't make enough to save. It's important to save something for retirement. If you can do that on a regular basis and make it your priority, it's important that you do so. As I look back, there are a lot of things we bought that we didn't have to. And even if you save a little something every week, on a regular basis, it will add up.

You may not feel like you have enough sometimes.
But remember, you have pride,
and you must keep it.

Finding Uncle J.D.

A phone call can change your life for bad and for good. Our lives changed in June of 1987 when my mother learned that her baby brother was alive. Uncle J.D. left Mississippi when I was 17 years old. I'm not sure if he tried to get in touch before then or not, but since my mother had lived in several states over the 42 years, they were out of touch, maybe he couldn't reach her. Anyhow, she thought he was dead, but he wasn't. My mother was in shock and would not believe the news until she talked to him herself. We stayed all night waiting for messages to be left and phone lines to connect. It was an exciting time, and it brought our family together in new way. Uncle J.D. had never married and had no children. He lived in the valley of Yuma, Arizona, and of course, that gave us a reason to have a road trip.

On June 13, 1988, we took the train to visit him, and that was my first trip so far away from home. It was also my first train trip in over 40 years. I saw some interesting sights. I was afraid going through the mountains because the train looked as if we were going to flip over on those narrow tracks, especially through the deep long curves. I just started to pray for God to keep me safe. I knew that after this, I would never take a train through those mountains ever again. We went through Texarkana, Texas, San Antonio, and miles of large mountains and valleys. We crossed the Rio Grande River and hundreds of miles of mountains and dry land. Finally on June 15th, we arrived in Yuma, Arizona.

Uncle J.D

Uncle J.D. met us at the station, and he was doing fine. They have a lot of cactus and palm trees growing there, and the weather was a very hot 109 degrees. We drove through Dome Valley, a large mountain range, on the way to Uncle J.D.'s home. One day the temperature was 112 degrees. That was the first time I had ever been in that kind of temperature. The humidity wasn't as bad as ours in the Midwest, so I believe that's why I could stand it. But what can you really say? It was hot! On our way back to St. Louis we passed many historical sites including 5,000 retired airplanes in a hunk of desert outside Tuscan.

At Benson, AZ, they had the largest cavalry fought in the United States by Negroes. Fort Huachuca has served as home of the famous Negro troops, the Buffalo Soldiers, who, among other exploits, chased Pancho Villa. We also passed a Montezuma Castle, which is built into a cliff, located between Phoenix and Flagstaff. The castle had 20 rooms and a dungeon.

In 1990, when we went to visit Uncle J.D. again, we traveled by car, which made me feel more comfortable. We stopped near Flagstaff, in an Indian town, and I bought a Turquoise ring for $25.00 and a few other items. When we arrived in Flagstaff, it was snowing very hard, and we had to stay overnight in a motel. We arrived to my uncle's house, and he was doing fine. We had good communication, and while we were there, my brother helped our uncle move into another trailer.

The temperature was much cooler this trip because it was November, with highs in the 80s and lows in the 50s. It was very dusty there, and it had not rained in a long time. They were harvesting lettuce and cantaloupes and getting the soil ready for replanting. They had to irrigate their land to grow vegetables. I noticed a lot of citrus trees with fruit on them, lemons, limes, and oranges. After returning home, I wrote my uncle a letter thanking him for the love he shared with us. He kept in touch with my mother every month, and since he knew his sister was a widow and 83 years old by that time, he helped her financially, too.

I received a call from my daughter, Linda, around 4am one morning in July 1991 saying something was wrong with her husband, my son-in-law William Harvey. She had called the paramedics, but it was too late. He had died of a massive heart attack. Right after his funeral I received a call from Arizona stating that uncle J.D. was found dead in his home. My mother, Rufus, and her grandson, Gary Lee, drove to Yuma. Someone told me that the minister stopped speaking during the burial because the wind blew his check out of the Bible at the moment he said, "Dust to dust, ashes to ashes." My uncle was buried in Welton, Arizona.

When he decided to find her, not only did his choice fill a space in my mother's heart, it also lead the way for more love, more experiences and more world experience through travel for me and my brothers. It's important to be in touch with your family and friends because through them can be unexpected and welcomed blessings.

You must prepare for the future. This includes paying for your funeral and for your living during retirement. Realize that and start early in life to build your security, and stay in touch with family.

The 1990s

The '90s were a trying time for my family. Lots of things happened, some tragic, some happy. My husband retired in 1991 at the age of 65. My oldest granddaughter married. It was a large wedding, and family members who lived out of town were able to attend. We had a family gathering to discuss a family reunion that was to be held in Memphis. We pulled it off, and it was a great time.

In March 1992, my husband, our son, Paul, and I were on our way back from Memphis visiting my mother. When we got to our house, the police were all over our home; they were looking for Paul. They told us a crime had been committed during the time we were all in Memphis. Although Paul traveled to Memphis with the family, he was not with us when we arrived home because we dropped him off at a friend's house. I asked the police to tell me what my son was accused of doing, but they would not tell me. My son happened to call the house during this time, and I told him the police were looking for him and that they were harassing his father and me. My son told me, "Mother, I will turn myself into the police."

My son was accused of a crime that occurred in Wentzville, MO, a city in St. Charles County, where there are not a lot of blacks. They made my son out to be a criminal, but they did not have enough evidence of the crime they accused him of doing. It did not matter to the authorities. I prayed to God to please have mercy on all of us, to give me endurance and to give my son justice. Paul was the youngest of our nine children. He was 29 years old at the time this all happened.

My husband had always provided a home for his family through good times and hard times. He was independent and had taken responsibility for his family at all times. We believe in good morals, honesty, truth, kindness, mildness and self-control. But this situation with my son was different. The way he was treated, the way we were treated and how things happened was very traumatic for us all. We weren't prepared because we had not had to deal with the law or authorities like that. The sad thing was that it was obvious that they were not treating us fairly, and we didn't know what to do about it at the time. Had we had some experience or real help, maybe things would have turned out differently.

A little over a year later, in October 1993, my son's trial was held. I prayed that God would bless this trial. The trial was unfair and based on the color of my son's skin. I experienced long-suffering and prayed for Jehovah to give me faith. Have mercy. We saw our son come through in handcuffs, and his legs were shackled. He called out to his father and me as he passed us, and he said, "I am not guilty." Tears rolled down my face. They told us to sit on a bench outside the trial door, and they put newspaper up to the glass door so we could not see what they were doing. My husband and I felt helpless. We were the only blacks there, and all of the jurors were white. We sat on that bench for hours. I thought to myself, "I couldn't believe this is happening." The jury found my son guilty.

I was devastated. The thought of anyone going to prison was awful, let alone my son. It was degrading, and he was in Memphis with us when they say that crime happened. That is a fact. I realize that his sentence was about more than the crime that he was accused of. It was about the color of his skin and his choice of a girlfriend. She was white and the mother of his four children. That is when his trouble began. I tried to tell him what was going on, but I could not get him to see it. He would tell me I was wrong. He said, "It's not like the old times mother. They have changed. Everyone is equal." When the police would see her in his car, they would always stop him. I call it harassing him. When their twins were born, the police stopped them on their way home from the hospital. Naturally, my son was angry. They took him out of the car and to jail. They did not charge him with anything; they just kept him there and released him later. His car was towed because they would not let the girl drive his car. She had to walk home with her newborn twins along with the two other children who were in the car. And it was very cold and dark. When I found out, I called the police station and asked why they didn't let the girl drive the car. They laughed and said, "Oh, she wanted to walk home." The harassment did not stop until they charged him with the crime in March 1992.

In the middle of the situation with my Paul, my great-grandson, Terrance L. Ramsey, whom we raised, was shot. It was December 1992, and I went to the scene where Terrance had been shot by a police officer. One of the officers at the scene told me that the shooting was justifiable. How could he say that when the investigation had not even begun? It hurt so bad to hear the officer say that. My heart was so heavy.

The police told me they were taking me to the hospital when they put me in a patrol car. Over the radio in the car, I heard someone say, "Don't take her to the hospital. Take her to my office downtown." I asked the officers if they were talking about me and they said, "Yes." I told them I was told at the scene that I was to be taken to the hospital and a detective would meet me there. It was dark by that time. They kept me downtown for two, maybe three hours. I kept asking why they were keeping me and how was my grandson. No one knew any information. I did not like this. I had to sit in a room with male police officers who were cursing. They put me in a room that had a sign that read "prisoner" on it. I knocked on the door to ask if I was under arrest because of what the sign on the door read. I asked, "Please, do you have any information about my grandson?" I was getting paranoid. I felt like my civil rights were being violated. I wanted my husband and children. I could feel my blood pressure rising. No one had any information. I don't know how long I sat there, then the detective who was supposed to meet me at the hospital walked by and said, "I thought you were meeting me at the hospital." I told him, "I thought so too, but this is where I ended up. No one will tell me anything. You say that you just left the hospital. Please, tell me, is Terrance dead or alive?" The detective told me he was dead. I have never been arrested in my life. Why was I held downtown at the jail?

As a mother and grandmother to this family, I try to practice love at all times.

"Love is long-suffering and kind; it bears all things, believes all things, and hopes all things, love never falls."—1 Corinthians 13:4-8.

Taking Care of Mother Kay

When she was 86 years old, I brought my mother, Mrs. Kay Nelson, to St. Louis to stay a while with me because she could no longer stay alone at her house in Memphis. She had lost most of her short term memory. Still eating well, she was not on any medication. Mother liked to go out on the patio every day. She also went to my garden to get flowers for fresh bouquets. I was still working a full-time job at that time and couldn't take time with mother like I felt I should. My oldest daughter, Regina, lived with us during that time. She cooked and cared for my mother while I worked. Mother looked for me every day, and all day she knocked on my husband's door asking for Elouise, calling me by my middle name. She always talked about when she was a child and her father and mother. She talked about when her oldest sister, Annie, got married. She would repeatedly state that it was a very big wedding held at their home. At that time, they had a large two-story house with a large back and front porch. She said an old lady cousin of theirs kept repeating, "That's the prettiest bride I ever seen," while she was just fanning herself.

By that time, my husband has been retired for four years. Wilmer had high blood pressure, asthma and diabetes. I had to give him insulin shots three times a day. My mother continued to knock on my husband's door asking for me but never complained, not even once. My daughter felt sorry for her grandmother because she didn't know who she was due to memory loss. At times mother could be humorous, unusual and unique. I still respected my mother and felt so helpless that there was nothing I could do about her mind. She asked me often about what was wrong. She said there was something wrong with her senses, and she didn't know what it was or what was causing it. Sometimes she thought she was going crazy. She just wanted to know what was happening to her.

Mrs. Kay Nelson, My Dear Mother

At 89-years-old, mother began saying, "Where shall I go? What shall I do?" She didn't always know who I was, and that hurt me. She would laugh with the children, although she didn't know that they were her grandchildren, great-grandchildren and great-great-grandchildren. When they told her who they were, she would tell them, "I'll be a son of a snake doctor." She never forgot where she was born. She knew the city, state and country. She was still walking and eating on her own and also enjoyed the gardens that I continued to plant for her.

I retired from Christian Northeast hospital in June of 1996. Thank God for that day! He gave me many, many years of punching the clock in order to make a living to help my husband with our family. Sometimes I would ask my God how long I could survive on a job with a home and children to take care of. But you know Jehovah God is good. He made a way for our family, sometimes up, sometimes down, sometimes pain and sometimes good. How wonderful He is! He gave me endurance to tolerate many different personalities; he gave me kindness, mildness, and self-control. And then He gave me retirement. I remain grateful and thankful.

Aging and Everyday Living

My husband and I always worked to take care of our family. Once we were both retired, it was still a struggle to survive. My only hope was to believe and have faith in Jehovah God, who helped me to survive the many trials and tribulations of my life. No matter how hard it gets, I am not done yet.

Wilmer and Martha, Life-Long Love

Wilmer was told in June 1999 that he had esophageal cancer and COPD. He refused to have surgery, chemotherapy and radiation because of his asthma, high blood pressure and diabetes. Prior to the diagnoses, my sister, Barbara, died in Baton Rouge. It was a year of sorrow for me. My truth in Jehovah God continued to give me strength to endure.

In January 2000, my husband was admitted to the hospital with pneumonia and was put on life support for three or four days. A week later, he was sent home. While Wilmer was in the hospital, my oldest brother, Rufus, fell dead from a heart attack in front of St. Mary's Hospital in East St. Louis, Illinois.

I had to take care of Rufus' arrangements because I had his Power of Attorney. No one else in my family could do it; he did not have a wife and my mother, who was 93 by then, could not help with her son. So while my husband was lying unconscious in the hospital, I had to leave his side to make arrangements to have my brother's body removed from the hospital. My children visited their father in hospital while I made funeral arrangements and cleaned out Rufus' apartment. Death just seemed to be around me because a few weeks later, my nephew in Memphis died. My husband was able to come home from the hospital, although he still had pneumonia. I was hopeful that he would be okay, but my loving husband died on March 28, 2000. It seemed like my heart stopped. We were married 52 years and 9 months. We did everything together. I just felt alone and numb. I wanted us to be 80 together, but all I could was to pray to Jehovah God to help me.

In honor of my husband, Mr. Wilmer H. Ramsey, our oldest granddaughter, Tabatha, whom my husband called Pumkin, wrote this tribute for her grandfather's obituary:

P – Precious is our lives always

U – Us, as grandchildren, will always remember.

M – Meaning more than you will ever know.

K – Kind words that you always said to me.

I – Important person that you will always be to me.

N – Now He lays you down to sleep. I pray the Lord your soul to keep.

From your loving granddaughter, TABBY!

Tabatha Milton-Rush, First-Born Granddaughter

I am living as a widow. Life without my husband is hard. I know many women who have lost their husbands before I lost mine, including my mother, who was widowed twice. Life is taking a different journey for me now. I am learning how to do things without my husband. We have lost the head of our family. We had some hard times and good times together.

My beloved husband was a loving, kind, humble and tenderly compassionate person. He never harmed anyone, and he had a very good heart. I loved him dearly, and I will cherish his memory. I miss him a lot.

A New Century

September 11, 2001, America was attacked by terrorists at the World Trade Center in New York and at the Pentagon in Washington, D.C. I was 71 years old when that happened. It seems that this country had lost it morals, honesty and respect for one another. I prayed for peace when that happened. Thank goodness people united together after that, for a little while, at least.

During my life, I felt that I encountered inequalities every day. I paid the highest interest rates, utilities, mortgage and taxes. I was born in this country. My parents and their parents were born in this country. My husband and sons served in the military. I still pray for change.

A few months later, when I woke up, I found that I could hardly move my right leg, and my right knee was swollen. At first, I didn't tell anyone of my children. The only person I had always depended on was my husband. Oh, how I missed him. I started to cry because I thought that I may be having a stroke, and my husband was not here with me. I could hardly walk for two days, so I pushed myself, and I even fell in my front yard. My knee just gave out. I had to have help to get up. Two weeks later, I went to see my doctor. She said I have arthritis. I am taking medicine, and it seems to be a crippling disease. Nothing has ever stopped me from walking. This was a frightening experience for me.

It took me about three years to adjust to being a widow. It has been about ??? years. All I have now are memories. I am thinking back; my husband and I were married 53 years. We had nine children. It was a hard struggle, but we made it. I prayed all the time. The way seemed very dark at times, doors closed on us at times, things were unfair, sometimes we didn't know where to turn, but we made it. With love, faith, pride, honor and truth we made it.

Fifty-three years is a long time together. We did so many things together, like going out to eat or going to the park. I can't talk to him anymore. I can't cook for him anymore. I can't look at or touch him anymore. All I have now are memories of our good and bad times. I could endure anything with my husband by my side. The house was so silent. I missed the sound of his voice, even in a world full of noise.

My mother, Kay Z Nelson, died in my home on April 8, 2003. When that happened, I really felt alone; I couldn't really describe it. Yes, I had children and plenty of grandchildren and great-grandchildren, but they couldn't take the place of a husband or mother. My trust stayed in Jehovah God, as I knew He would take care of me and help me to endure the pain.

I received a call that my baby brother, Savage, had lung cancer. I was able to visit Savage in Memphis. It had been eight years since I last visited him. Tears were in my eyes as I looked at Savage. He was very thin and weak, but he was holding his own. While I was there I was able to see my daughters and two more of my brothers and others at a big fish fry that my niece and her husband had at their house.

I lost my son, Gregory, in August 2006, at the age of 52. He had been in poor health for about 15 years. For three years, he was using a walker. He was able to take care of himself and live on his own. I looked forward to his daily calls to see how I was doing. He had been checking on me since my husband died. I love all of my children, and a part of me left when Gregory died. I can't help by cry sometimes when I think about my husband and son, but I know I must go on for all of my other children. They keep me on my toes.

Changing Times

I have been a person that people could rely on. If I promise to do something, I will always do my best to do it, or help someone if I could help them. My family seemed to depend on me for everything. I tell them, Never say I can't; say I will." I have always found solutions to my problems by my faith in God. I always find a way through any situation. I try to be positive.

I think often about Matthew 6:31, 32: "*Therefore do not be anxious, saying, 'What shall we eat?' or 'What shall we drink?' or 'What shall we wear?' For the Gentiles seek after all these things, and your heavenly Father knows that you need them all." (*English Standard Version)

I know the world is changing, but that doesn't mean values should. Some of my grandchildren disagree with me and reward me with bad values for good. With the changing times, some think that they don't have to work hard or take responsibility. I am trying to do well, yet they are resisting me. I think, "Do not be overcome by evil, but overcome evil with good." (Romans 12:21, ESV). I have experienced a lot of things in life they know nothing about. I have done some things I would not repeat because I used bad judgment, but I learned from mistakes. I am not perfect, but I have always tried to do well and obey the rules.

My mother and grandfather taught me the beliefs, morals, honesty and spiritual values that shaped my life. Many of their philosophies and ideals guide me through life. My mother was an inspiration to me as I struggled through life raising my children. I share these with my grandchildren.

I have tried to teach my children, grandchildren and great-grands how to make the right choices in life. I know they can succeed if they use good judgment. I encourage them to do their best and to take care of their bodies by not smoking, drinking or doing drugs. Personally, I never wanted to do these things because of my mother's influence on me. I want to respect their space and trust them, but influence them in the right way. I love them all, and I just want to protect them. I always emphasize responsibility, accountability, decency and self-control.

When it comes to living as a role model for my kids and my community, I live by example. I am a private person, very family-oriented. I started taking some classes mainly so that my grandchildren will know that you never get too old to learn. I plan to take computer classes as well. I have to stay focused because everything is changing; nothing is the same anymore. I would die a happy person if all of the males in my family could all have jobs to take care of themselves and their children. I want my family to stop, think and set goals, be competitive and do their best. I want them to be supportive of others and be active doing community service. I always put myself last because I have a heart for others, so I am always extending a helping hand.

I have had to live my life following someone else's rules, my parents' guidance and society's laws. My grandchildren, great-grandchildren and great-great grandchildren don't want to follow rules. I have put up rules around the house as a reminder for my grandchildren because some of them have lived with me. I asked them to not smoke, drink heavily or curse in my house. I expect them to dress decent, show love, be kind and respect the grandmother who started this family of over 100. Things have changed over the last 20 years with this new generation. So, I had to let some of my grandchildren and children know their behavior is unacceptable, and if you disrespect my rules, we need to talk about the consequences. I expect them to be honest, responsible and trustworthy. I expect my children and grandchildren to respect and obey my rules. A mother who loves her children will lovingly discipline them. I love my family.

I also believe it's important to share. My children had to share things. We are a sharing family. Things that I have and own have to be shared. That's part of the love I share with them.

Whatever challenges may be in your future, pray for the strength to endure. Have compassion and self-control. You may be alone, but don't get lonely. When you feel lonely, try writing or reading something. Push negative thoughts out of your mind. I don't worry about tomorrow because my faith in my Bible tells me that I don't have to worry about the next day, for the Heavenly Father knows my needs. I awake every morning, open my door and think of the wonders of creation, the beautiful sunrise, a bird flying freely and the beautiful flowers blooming on the trees.

Stick Together and Have Faith

"Everything's gonna be alright"
– Wilmer H. Ramsey

I am a mother of nine. I learned early in their lives that I had nine different personalities to work with. As a mother, I love them all. They were my life. It was important to nurture and teach them to love one another, respect, to be honest, get along and communicate together. Everyone had to attend school and on Sundays and attend service.

With responsibilities and events in the world today, many have no natural affection. I think fathers should take responsibility for family. Nurture, cherish, love, protect them. Teach them to be polite, kind, honest, truthful, go to school and be obedient. Teach them to obey the laws, and let them know it's a system of rules to protect society and community.

Where but in the family do children form their first impressions of love, discipline and authority?

Parents who have taught those lessons successfully do so by making their homes of love, where they put away all anger, wrath and abusive speech, and teach their children vital lessons that will prepare them for life.

There are things you can do today that will give everyone a good future.

In order to make it, you must have some pride, self-esteem, be honest, trustworthy and have love in your heart. Get a mate that you trust, and be a mate that is trustworthy. Have faith and love because together you can make it. Also, obey the law of the country. These are the tools my husband and I had. We also respected people all our lives. Make goals for yourselves, think positive, live within your budget every day, save a few dollars and invest in a few stocks. Start saving for retirement early, as a little savings every month will build up more than you think. These are my experiences. Please think about them.

When I was growing up, we would help each other out. We should all love one another and our neighbors. Take care of next-door neighbors. Lending a hand to take care of their needs helps them to lend a hand and take care of yours, too.

Always go to church. Fathers and mothers should attend the services together because it is a family affair. Go somewhere where morals, truth, faith, love and discipline are being taught. It's necessary in bringing up a family because of the guidance given.

Kindness, honesty and sincerity go a long way.

Marriage, Communication and Faith

As a mother, I gave all of myself to the raising of my children. Everything I did was for them. I never thought of my needs, just of their needs. I even neglected my husband without realizing I was doing so. I also wanted their father, my husband, to do the same. I thought that's what parents should do. At the time, I thought he was being selfish at times because he wasn't catering to the children like I thought he should.

They were a part of us, and we chose to have them. They were my life until they became grownups. I was very happy with the rearing of my kids. It was such a pleasure for me to cook, clean the house, keep them clean, feed them, send them to school, attend their social activities and on Sunday, take them to attend service.

I never was tired of doing for my family. I thank God for giving me good health to take care of them. I am by no means perfect. When I was younger during my marriage, I had in my mind that I was always right. When it came to my husband, he had more ability than I realized. He just gave in to me and kept silent, which he should not have done. It took me years to realize what I was doing to myself.

When we married I was 17, and he was 21. He had been in the service, traveled the world and served our country. He really knew more about life and living than I could even imagine. I was kind of hotheaded and wanted things my way, and that wasn't right. As time passed and life happened, I learned to take time to listen and to take advice from him. I learned what it meant to work together and to make decisions together.

Even today, at 82 years old, I am trying hard to accept things and personalities, and I am trying not to change them. I give advice that I think is right but realize that I could be wrong, also. When you are married, it takes two people to communicate together. Don't be bullheaded and just do what you want to do. I learned the hard way. I learned to communicate better and work things out.

Faith is the key to sanity. Many times I thought of giving up, but keeping the faith in God keeps me going. No money can buy faith; everyone can have it for free.

Children Need Two Parents

"Fathers, love your wives more, and work with your children and communities more. Teach the children respect and honor. Be there for your family. It takes two to make the children and two to raise them."
– Mrs. Martha Ramsey

As you can tell, we've been through many ups and downs in our family. There have been times of accomplishment and also times of heartache, yet we knew we had to get through it. I can't imagine going through this long life without my husband. We were married for 53 years, and I miss him so very much. I also know that though we had low wages and tough times, we did it together, and our family is better for it.

Since I'm 82 years old, I don't mind telling you straight what's on my mind. Whatever you've done, it's okay.

You can always do better. I've made mistakes in my life, too. However, to get our society and our families back on track, we must all do something. It can start with you, where you are now. Make some changes if you need to because your children need you and so do those who love you.

For a family and togetherness, be married because children need two parents in the home. It's better to be married instead of just living together and raising kids or having kids without being married and not having both parents together, teaching, loving and sharing.

Parents that are married are as one. They should teach their children and give advice on the same level and let the children know they are loved. Children learn best with discipline and knowing they are cherished, protected and taught responsibilities by both parents. Since life is so different these days, it's even more important that we protect the children and teach them through nurturing and being responsible adults.

Married couples should stay together. Don't separate. Children need a mother and father in the home. That's what I had. Back when I was growing up, adults in the neighborhood would look out for your kids and protect them. That's not the case today, and your kids need you now more than ever.

Mothers, you need to have an interest in your children. Some mothers are so sad, afraid and messed up that they are killing their own children and themselves. I don't know what drives mothers to do that. It hurts me to see that. Raise your children through faith, and teach them how to honor and respect everyone. Mothers, please watch the way you dress.

"Watch what you do and say, and don't tolerate just any type of behavior."

Mother Kay's Wisdom

Just try to be a good person, good neighbor, good in the community, and get an education.

Do unto others as you would have them do unto you.

Make the most of what you are with pride.

Practice good behavior, good conduct and be honest.

Have compassion for human beings, love people and do for them because we are all connected.

Be truthful. Keep your words because your word is your bond.

"No matter where or how you start in life, stay the course and make the best of what you've been given."

– Mrs. Martha Ramsey

Closing Thoughts

I wonder why I'm still living while I have four children who are dead. I am grateful that five of them are alive. I have one brother still living. I'm so much older than they, and every one of my sisters is gone. I do realize some didn't take care of their health. Things like drinking heavy and that kind of "carrying on" don't help.

My children and grandchildren and great-grandchildren come to me for advice and ask me questions. When they have problems, they think I can solve them.

My husband and I started this family, and I've always tried to be responsible. I'll try to help where I can. I try to give and share what little I do have with them, especially my grandchildren. I try to treat them all alike, but some of them don't think so. I can't answer all the questions or settle all the things, but they think so.

This year I began to ask them, "When is my 'me' time?" I think some of them depend on me so much that they didn't become independent individuals like they should have. The reality is that I love them all, and I'll continue to do all I can as long as I am here. I think that's my duty to do that, and I've always enjoyed it. I just wish I could do more.

A NOTE FROM THE PUBLISHER

Mission Possible Press...
Creating Legacies through Absolute Good Works

As a publisher, I have the opportunity to transform hopeful writers into successful authors. This brings me great pleasure because I believe everyone has wisdom to share and valuable stories to tell.

Prior to publication, I worked with Mrs. Ramsey to help her take the meticulous notes from her life and craft them into the powerful wisdom you have experienced in these pages. Being the matriarch of such a large family, Mrs. Ramsey always has some news to report. During the completion of this book, just like her daily life, there were births, illnesses, victories and sadly, losses. Much like her aunt before her, Tabitha Milton-Rush, Mrs. Ramsey's oldest granddaughter, was murdered by a man she knew. It was hard on everyone because she was such a bright light in the world, and an encourager to her grandmother, eagerly awaiting her published book. Words just cannot describe the time...

Through it all however, Martha Ramsey practiced what she has shared – through faith, she continues to endure, and so shall we. Spending time with her was enlightening, warm and comforting – just like her.

Thanks to Mrs. Ramsey, we are continuing to make the *Mission Possible-creating legacies, inspiring and building up-especially for families.*

May your mind be sharpened, your heart be softened and your soul be lifted because you have been touched by a living, breathing precious spirit named Martha. I am honored and pleased to present this book as part of our Extraordinary Living Series.

In the Spirit of Communication,
Jo Lena Johnson, Founder and Publisher

Mission Possible Press, a division of Absolute Good
AbsoluteGoodBooks.com
MissionPossiblePress.com

ABOUT THE AUTHOR

Mrs. Martha Eloise Ramsey was born on a farm outside of Hazlehurst, Mississippi in 1930 and migrated to St. Louis, Missouri, with her husband, Wilmer Ramsey, and their children in the 1960s. Now a widow in her 80s with over 125 grand, great-grand and great-great-grand children, she shares wisdom and courage from her journey. She describes her life as having been good, and she remains grateful for the 53 years she was married to her husband, working on their same jobs to retirement, which allowed them to raise their children with steady employment. Appreciating the simple things in life, like nature and family, she loved being a wife and mother. Martha Ramsey started writing her story over 30 years ago because she wants readers to be strong and have courage.

ACKNOWLEDGEMENTS

My grateful thanks go to my baby daughter, Wanda Fay Ramsey Boyd, and my granddaughters, Pamela Ramsey and Nicole Ramsey, who encouraged me to finish this book. Thank you Alisha Peeples, my great-granddaughter, for taking my handwritten notes which started over 30 years ago, and "putting them into the computer" for me. My daughters, Linda Woods, Regina Mayweather and Sheila Ramsey, I thank you all.

I think back to when my husband and I were raising our children around 1963. A good Christian family came into our lives at a time when my husband was unemployed. They were like angels without any wings, blessing our lives with the most precious things. This family shared much love and kindness. Mrs. Maria Brown, the mother of that family, has been there for me through the deaths of my children and husband. She offered me sympathy, love and kindness. I have joyful, loving memories of my friend and

Friends, Maria and Martha

her family, her husband, James (deceased), and her son, Paul. In 2011, my best Christian friend turned 90 years old, and she is doing fine. Thank you so much.

I'd like to thank Jo Lena Johnson for making my book possible.

www.ingramcontent.com/pod-product-compliance
Lightning Source LLC
La Vergne TN
LVHW011030110826
845149LV00015B/3353

* 9 7 8 0 9 8 5 2 7 6 0 3 4 *